The Empire of Rome
AD 98–180

EDWARD GIBBON

A Phoenix Paperback

This edition first published in Great Britain by Phoenix
A division of Orion Books Ltd
Orion House, 5 Upper St Martin's Lane, London WC2H 9EA

Taken from chapters I and II of *The Decline and Fall of The Roman
Empire*

Cover illustration: The Coliseum, Rome; © Hulton Deutsch Collection

ISBN 1 85799 537 6

Typeset by Deltatype Ltd, Ellesmere Port, Cheshire
Printed in Great Britain by Clays Ltd, St Ives plc

I
(AD 98–180)

The extent and military force of the empire in the age of the Antonines

In the second century of the Christian era the empire of Rome comprehended the fairest part of the earth and the most civilized portion of mankind. The frontiers of that extensive monarchy were guarded by ancient renown and disciplined valour. The gentle but powerful influence of laws and manners had gradually cemented the union of the provinces. Their peaceful inhabitants enjoyed and abused the advantages of wealth and luxury. The image of a free constitution was preserved with decent reverence: the Roman senate appeared to possess the sovereign authority and devolved on the emperors all the executive powers of government. During a happy period of more than fourscore years, the public administration was conducted by the virtue and abilities of Nerva, Trajan, Hadrian, and the two Antonines. It is the design of this and of the two succeeding chapters to describe the prosperous condition of their empire, and afterwards, from the death of Marcus Antoninus, to deduce the most important circumstances of its decline and fall, a revolution which will ever be remembered and is still felt by the nations of the earth.

The principal conquests of the Romans were achieved under the republic; and the emperors, for the most part, were satisfied with preserving those dominions which had been acquired by the policy of the senate, the active emulation of the consuls, and the martial enthusiasm of the people. The seven first centuries were filled with a rapid succession of triumphs; but it was reserved for Augustus to relinquish the ambitious design of subduing the whole earth and to introduce a spirit of moderation into the public councils. Inclined to peace by his temper and situation, it was easy for him to discover that Rome, in her present exalted situation, had much less to hope than to fear from the chance of arms; and that, in the prosecution of remote wars, the undertaking became every day more difficult, the event more doubtful, and the possession more precarious and less beneficial. The experience of Augustus added weight to these salutary reflections and effectually convinced him that, by the prudent vigour of his counsels, it would be easy to secure every concession which the safety or the dignity of Rome might require from the most formidable barbarians. Instead of exposing his person and his legions to the arrows of the Parthians, he obtained, by an honourable treaty, the restitution of the standards and prisoners which had been taken in the defeat of Crassus.

His generals, in the early part of his reign, attempted the reduction of Æthiopia and Arabia Felix [Yemen]. They marched near a thousand miles to the south of the tropic;

but the heat of the climate soon repelled the invaders and protected the unwarlike natives of those sequestered regions. The northern countries of Europe scarcely deserved the expense and labour of conquest. The forests and morasses of Germany were filled with a hardy race of barbarians, who despised life when it was separated from freedom; and though on the first attack they seemed to yield to the weight of the Roman power, they soon, by a signal act of despair, regained their independence and reminded Augustus of the vicissitude of fortune. On the death of that emperor his testament was publicly read in the senate. He bequeathed, as a valuable legacy to his successors, the advice of confining the empire within those limits which Nature seemed to have placed as its permanent bulwarks and boundaries: on the west the Atlantic Ocean; the Rhine and Danube on the north; the Euphrates on the east; and towards the south, the sandy deserts of Arabia and Africa.

The only accession which the Roman empire received during the first century of the Christian era was the province of Britain. In this single instance the successors of Cæsar and Augustus were persuaded to follow the example of the former rather than the precept of the latter. The proximity of its situation to the coast of Gaul seemed to invite their arms; the pleasing though doubtful intelligence of a pearl fishery attracted their avarice; and as Britain was viewed in the light of a distinct and insulated world, the conquest scarcely formed any exception to the general system of continental measures. After a war of about forty years, undertaken by the most stupid, maintained by the most dissolute, and terminated by the most timid of all the emperors, the far greater part of the island submitted to the Roman yoke. The various tribes of Britons possessed valour without conduct, and the love of freedom without the spirit of union. They took up arms with savage fierceness; they laid them down or turned them against each other with wild inconstancy; and while they fought singly, they were successively subdued. Neither the fortitude of Caractacus, nor the despair of Boadicea, nor the fanaticism of the Druids, could avert the slavery of their country or resist the steady progress of the Imperial generals, who maintained the national glory when the throne was disgraced by the weakest or the most vicious of mankind. At the very time when Domitian, confined to his palace, felt the terrors which he inspired, his legions, under the command of the virtuous Agricola, defeated the collected force of the Caledonians at the foot of the Grampian hills; and his fleets, venturing to explore an unknown and dangerous navigation, displayed the Roman arms round every part of the island. The conquest of Britain was considered as already achieved; and it was the design of Agricola to complete and ensure his success by the easy reduction of Ireland, for which in his opinion one legion and a few auxiliaries were sufficient. The western isle might be improved into a valuable possession, and the Britons would wear their chains with the less reluctance if the prospect and example of freedom were on every side removed from before their eyes.

But the superior merit of Agricola soon occasioned his removal from the government of Britain, and forever disappointed this rational though extensive scheme of conquest. Before his departure the prudent general had provided for security as well as for dominion. He had observed that the island is almost divided into two unequal parts by the opposite gulfs or, as they are now called, the Firths of Scotland. Across the narrow interval of about forty miles he had drawn a line of military stations, which was afterwards fortified in the reign of Antoninus Pius by a turf rampart erected on foundations of stone. This wall of Antoninus, at a small distance beyond the modern cities of Edinburgh and Glasgow, was fixed as the limit of the Roman province. The native Caledonians preserved in the northern extremity of the island their wild independence, for which they were not less indebted to their poverty than to their valour. Their incursions were frequently repelled and chastised, but their country was never subdued. The masters of the fairest and most wealthy climates of the globe turned with contempt from gloomy hills assailed by the winter tempest, from lakes concealed in a blue mist, and from cold and lonely heaths over which the deer of the forest were chased by a troop of naked barbarians.

Such was the state of the Roman frontiers, and such the maxims of Imperial policy, from the death of Augustus to the accession of Trajan. That virtuous and active prince had received the education of a soldier and possessed the talents of a general. The peaceful system of his predecessors was interrupted by scenes of war and conquest; and the legions, after a long interval, beheld a military emperor at their head. The first exploits of Trajan were against the Dacians, the most warlike of men, who dwelt beyond the Danube, and who, during the reign of Domitian, had insulted with impunity the majesty of Rome. To the strength and fierceness of barbarians they added a contempt for life, which was derived from a warm persuasion of the immortality and transmigration of the soul. Decebalus, the Dacian king, approved himself a rival not unworthy of Trajan; nor did he despair of his own and the public fortune till, by the confession of his enemies, he had exhausted every resource both of valour and policy. This memorable war, with a very short suspension of hostilities, lasted five years; and as the emperor could exert without control the whole force of the state, it was terminated by an absolute submission of the barbarians. The new province of Dacia, which formed a second exception to the precept of Augustus, was about thirteen hundred miles in circumference. Its natural boundaries were the Dniester, the Theiss or Tibiscus, the Lower Danube, and the Euxine Sea [Black Sea]. The vestiges of a military road may still be traced from the banks of the Danube to the neighbourhood of Bender, a place famous in modern history, and the actual frontier of the Turkish and Russian empires.

Trajan was ambitious of fame; and as long as mankind shall continue to bestow more liberal applause on their destroyers than on their benefactors, the thirst of military glory will ever be the vice of the most exalted characters. The praises of Alexander, transmitted by a succession of poets and historians, had kindled a dangerous emulation in the mind of Trajan. Like him, the Roman emperor undertook an expedition against the nations of the East, but he lamented with a sigh that his advanced age scarcely left him any hopes of equalling the renown of the son of Philip. Yet the success of Trajan, however transient, was rapid and specious. The degenerate Parthians, broken by intestine discord, fled before his arms. He descended the river Tigris in triumph, from the mountains of Armenia to the Persian gulf. He enjoyed the honour of being the first, as he was the last, of the Roman generals who ever navigated that remote sea. His fleets ravaged the coasts of Arabia; and Trajan vainly flattered himself that he was approaching towards the confines of India. Every day the astonished senate received the intelligence of new names and new nations that acknowledged his sway. But the death of Trajan soon clouded the splendid prospect; and it was justly to be dreaded that so many distant nations would throw off the unaccustomed yoke when they were no longer restrained by the powerful hand which had imposed it.

It was an ancient tradition that when the Capitol was founded by one of the Roman kings, the god Terminus (who presided over boundaries and was represented according to the fashion of that age by a large stone) alone among all the inferior deities refused to yield his place to

Jupiter himself. A favourable inference was drawn from his obstinacy, which was interpreted by the augurs as a sure presage that the boundaries of the Roman power would never recede. During many ages the prediction, as it is usual, contributed to its own accomplishment. But though Terminus had resisted the majesty of Jupiter, he submitted to the authority of the emperor Hadrian. The resignation of all the eastern conquests of Trajan was the first measure of his reign. He restored to the Parthians the election of an independent sovereign, withdrew the Roman garisons from the provinces of Armenia, Mesopotamia, and Assyria, and in compliance with the precept of Augustus once more established the Euphrates as the frontier of the empire.

The martial and ambitious spirit of Trajan formed a very singular contrast with the moderation of his successor. The restless activity of Hadrian was not less remarkable when compared with the gentle repose of Antoninus Pius. The life of the former was almost a perpetual journey; and as he possessed the various talents of the soldier, the statesman, and the scholar, he gratified his curiosity in the discharge of his duty. Careless of the difference of seasons and of climates, he marched on foot and bareheaded over the snows of Caledonia and the sultry plains of the Upper Egypt; nor was there a province of the empire which, in the course of his reign, was not honoured with the presence of the monarch. But the tranquil life of Antoninus Pius was spent in the bosom of Italy; and during the twenty-three

years that he directed the public administration the longest journeys of that amiable prince extended no farther than from his palace in Rome to the retirement of his Lanuvian villa.

Notwithstanding this difference in their personal conduct, the general system of Augustus was equally adopted and uniformly pursued by Hadrian and by the two Antonines. They persisted in the design of maintaining the dignity of the empire without attempting to enlarge its limits. By every honourable expedient they invited the friendship of the barbarians and endeavoured to convince mankind that the Roman power, raised above the temptation of conquest, was actuated only by the love of order and justice. During a long period of forty-three years their virtuous labours were crowned with success; and if we except a few slight hostilities that served to exercise the legions of the frontier, the reigns of Hadrian and Antoninus Pius offer the fair prospect of universal peace. The Roman name was revered among the most remote nations of the earth. The fiercest barbarians frequently submitted their differences to the arbitration of the emperor; and we are informed by a contemporary historian that he had seen ambassadors who were refused the honour, which they came to solicit, of being admitted into the rank of subjects.

The terror of the Roman arms added weight and dignity to the moderation of the emperors. They preserved peace by a constant preparation for war; and while justice regulated their conduct, they announced to the nations on their confines that they were as little disposed to endure as to offer an injury. The military strength which it had been sufficient for Hadrian and the elder Antoninus to display was exerted against the Parthians and the Germans by the emperor Marcus. The hostilities of the barbarians provoked the resentment of that philosophic monarch, and in the prosecution of a just defence Marcus and his generals obtained many signal victories both on the Euphrates and on the Danube. The military establishment of the Roman empire, which thus assured either its tranquillity or success, will now become the proper and important object of our attention.

In the purer ages of the commonwealth the use of arms was reserved for those ranks of citizens who had a country to love, a property to defend, and some share in enacting those laws which it was their interest as well as duty to maintain. But in proportion as the public freedom was lost in extent of conquest, war was gradually improved into an art and degraded into a trade. The legions themselves, even at the time when they were recruited in the most distant provinces, were supposed to consist of Roman citizens. That distinction was generally considered either as a legal qualification or as a proper recompense for the soldier; but a more serious regard was paid to the essential merit of age, strength, and military stature. In all levies a just preference was given to the climates of the North over those of the South; the race of men born to the exercise of arms was sought for in the country rather than in cities; and it was very reasonably presumed that the hardy occupations of smiths, carpenters, and huntsmen would supply more vigour and resolution than the sedentary trades which are employed in the service of luxury. After every qualification of property had been laid aside, the armies of the Roman emperors were still commanded for the most part by officers of a liberal birth and education; but the common soldiers, like the mercenary troops of modern Europe, were drawn from the meanest and very frequently from the most profligate of mankind.

That public virtue which among the ancients was denominated patriotism is derived from a strong sense of our own interest in the preservation and prosperity of the free government of which we are members. Such a sentiment, which had rendered the legions of the republic almost invincible, could make but a very feeble impression on the mercenary servants of a despotic prince; and it became necessary to supply that defect by other motives of a different but not less forcible nature – honour and religion. The peasant or mechanic imbibed the useful prejudice that he was advanced to the more dignified profession of arms, in which his rank and reputation would depend on his own valour; and that, although the prowess of a private soldier must often escape the notice of fame, his own behaviour might sometimes confer glory or disgrace on the company, the legion, or even the army to whose honours he was associated. On his first entrance into the service an oath was administered to him with every circumstance of solemnity. He promised never to desert his standard, to submit his own will to the commands of his leaders, and to sacrifice his life for the safety of the emperor and the empire. The attachment of the Roman troops to their standards was inspired by the united influence of religion and of honour. The golden eagle which glittered in the front of the legion was the object of their fondest devotion; nor was it esteemed less impious than it was ignominious to abandon that sacred ensign in the hour of danger. These motives, which derived their strength from the imagination, were enforced by fears and hopes of a more substantial kind. Regular pay, occasional donatives, and a stated recompense after the appointed time of service alleviated the hardships of the military life, whilst on the other hand it was impossible for cowardice or disobedience to escape the severest punishment. The centurions were authorized to chastise with blows, the generals had a right to punish with death; and it was an inflexible maxim of Roman discipline that a good soldier should dread his officers far more than the enemy. From such laudable arts did the valour of the Imperial troops receive a degree of firmness and docility unattainable by the impetuous and irregular passions of barbarians.

And yet so sensible were the Romans of the imperfection of valour without skill and practice that in their language the name of an army was borrowed from the word which signified exercise. Military exercises were the important and unremitted object of their discipline. The recruits and young soldiers were constantly trained both in the morning and in the evening, nor was age or knowledge allowed to excuse the veterans from the daily repetition of what they had completely learned. Large sheds were erected in the winter-quarters of the troops that their useful labours might not receive any interruption from the most tempestuous weather; and it was carefully observed that the arms destined to this imitation of war should be of double the weight which was required in real action.

We have attempted to explain the spirit which moderated and the strength which supported the power of Hadrian and the Antonines. We shall now endeavour with clearness and precision to describe the provinces once united under their sway but at present divided into so many independent and hostile states.

Spain, the western extremity of the empire, of Europe, and of the ancient world, has in every age invariably preserved the same natural limits: the Pyrenæan mountains, the Mediterranean, and the Atlantic Ocean. That great peninsula, at present so unequally divided between two sovereigns, was distributed by Augustus into three provinces, Lusitania, Bætica, and Tarraconensis. The kingdom of Portugal now fills the place of the warlike country of the Lusitanians; and the loss sustained by the former on the side of the east is compensated by an accession of territory towards the north. The confines of Grenada and Andalusia correspond with those of ancient Bætica. The remainder of Spain, Galicia and the Asturias, Biscay and Navarre, León and the two Castilles, Murcia, Valencia, Catalonia, and Aragon, all contributed to form the third and most 13 considerable of the Roman governments, which from the name of its capital was styled the province of Tarragona. Of the native barbarians, the Celtiberians were the most powerful, as the Cantabrians and Asturians proved the most obstinate. Confident in the strength of their mountains, they were the last who submitted to the arms of Rome and the first who threw off the yoke of the Arabs.

Ancient Gaul, as it contained the whole country between the Pyrenees, the Alps, the Rhine, and the Ocean, was of greater extent than modern France. To the dominions of that powerful monarchy, with its recent acquisitions of Alsace and Lorraine, we must add the duchy of Savoy, the cantons of Switzerland, the four electorates of the Rhine, and the territories of Liége, Luxembourg, Hainault, Flanders and Brabant. When Augustus gave laws to the conquests of his father, he introduced a division of Gaul equally adapted to the progress of the legions, to the course of the rivers, and to the principal national distinctions, which had comprehended above an hundred independent states. The seacoast of the Mediterranean, Languedoc, Provence, and Dauphiné, received their provincial appellation from the colony of Narbonne. The government of Aquitaine was extended from the Pyrenees to the Loire. The country between the Loire and the Seine was styled the Celtic Gaul, and soon borrowed a new denomination from the celebrated colony of Lugdunum, or Lyons. The Belgic lay beyond the Seine, and in more ancient times had been bounded only by the Rhine; but a little before the age of

Cæsar the Germans, abusing their superiority of valour, had occupied a considerable portion of the Belgic territory. The Roman conquerors very eagerly embraced so flattering a circumstance, and the Gallic frontier of the Rhine, from Basel to Leyden, received the pompous names of the Upper and the Lower Germany. Such, under the reign of the Antonines, were the six provinces of Gaul: the Narbonnese, Aquitaine, the Celtic or Lyonnese, the Belgic, and the two Germanies.

We have already had occasion to mention the conquest of Britain and to fix the boundary of the Roman province in this island. It comprehended all England, Wales, and the Lowlands of Scotland as far as Dumbarton and Edinburgh. Before Britain lost her freedom the country was irregularly divided between thirty tribes of barbarians, of whom the most considerable were the Belgæ in the West, the Brigantes in the North, the Silures in South Wales, and the Iceni in Norfolk and Suffolk. As far as we can either trace or credit the resemblance of manners and language, Spain, Gaul, and Britain were peopled by the same hardy race of savages. Before they yielded to the Roman arms, they often disputed the field, and often renewed the contest. After their submission they constituted the western division of the European provinces, which extended from the columns of Hercules to the wall of Antoninus, and from the mouth of the Tagus to the sources of the Rhine and Danube.

Before the Roman conquest the country which is now called Lombardy was not considered as a part of Italy. It had been occupied by a powerful colony of Gauls, who, settling themselves along the banks of the Po from Piedmont to Romagna, carried their arms and diffused their name from the Alps to the Apennine. The Ligurians dwelt on the rocky coast which now forms the republic of Genoa. Venice was yet unborn; but the territories of that state, which lie to the east of the Adige, were inhabited by the Venetians. The middle part of the peninsula that now composes the duchy of Tuscany and the ecclesiastical state was the ancient seat of the Etruscans and Umbrians, to the former of whom Italy was indebted for the first rudiments of civilized life. The Tiber rolled at the foot of the seven hills of Rome, and the country of the Sabines, the Latins, and the Volsci, from that river to the frontiers of Naples, was the theatre of her infant victories. On that celebrated ground the first consuls deserved triumphs, their successors adorned villas, and *their* posterity have erected convents. Capua and Campania possessed the immediate territory of Naples; the rest of the kingdom was inhabited by many warlike nations, the Marsi, the Samnites, the Apulians, and the Lucanians; and the seacoasts had been covered by the flourishing colonies of the Greeks. We may remark that when Augustus divided Italy into eleven regions the little province of Istria was annexed to that seat of Roman sovereignty.

The European provinces of Rome were protected by the course of the Rhine and the Danube. The latter of those mighty streams, which rises at the distance of only thirty miles from the former, flows above thirteen hundred miles, for the most part to the southeast, collects the tribute of sixty navigable rivers, and is at length, through six mouths, received into the Euxine, which appears scarcely equal to such an accession of waters. The provinces of the Danube soon acquired the general appellation of Illyricum, or the Illyrian frontier, and were esteemed the most warlike of the empire; but they deserve to be more particularly considered under the names of Rhætia, Noricum, Pannonia, Dalmatia, Dacia, Mæsia, Thrace, Macedonia, and Greece.

The province of Rhætia, which soon extinguished the name of the Vindelicians, extended from the summit of the Alps to the banks of the Danube; from its source, as far as its conflux with the Inn. The greatest part of the flat country is subject to the elector of Bavaria; the city of Augsburg is protected by the constitution of the German empire; the Grisons are safe in their mountains, and the country of Tyrol is ranked among the numerous provinces of the house of Austria.

The wide extent of territory which is included between the Inn, the Danube, and the Save – Austria, Styria, Carinthia, Carniola, the Lower Hungary, and Sclavonia – was known to the ancients under the names of Noricum and Pannonia. In their original state of independence, their fierce inhabitants were intimately connected. Under the Roman government they were frequently united, and they still remain the patrimony of a single family. They now contain the residence of a German prince, who styles himself Emperor of the Romans, and form the centre as well as strength of the Austrian power. It may not be improper to observe that if we except Bohemia, Moravia, the northern skirts of Austria, and a part of Hungary between the Theiss and the Danube, all the other dominions of the house of Austria were comprised within the limits of the Roman empire.

Dalmatia, to which the name of Illyricum more properly belonged, was a long but narrow tract between the Save and the Adriatic. The best part of the seacoast, which still retains its ancient appellation, is a province of the Venetian state and the seat of the little republic of Ragusa. The inland parts have assumed the Sclavonian names of Croatia and Bosnia; the former obeys an Austrian governor, the latter a Turkish pasha; but the whole country is still infested by tribes of barbarians whose savage independence irregularly marks the doubtful limit of the Christian and Mahometan power.

After the Danube had received the waters of the Theiss and the Save, it acquired, at least among the Greeks, the name of Ister. It formerly divided Mæsia and Dacia, the latter of which, as we have already seen, was a conquest of Trajan, and the only province beyond the river. If we inquire into the present state of those countries, we shall find that, on the left hand of the Danube, Temeswar and Transylvania have been annexed, after many revolutions, to the crown of Hungary; whilst the principalities of Moldavia and Wallachia acknowledge the supremacy of the Ottoman Porte. On the right hand of the Danube, Mæsia, which during the middle ages was broken into the barbarian kingdoms of Servia and Bulgaria, is again united in Turkish slavery.

The appellation of Roumelia, which is still bestowed by the Turks on the extensive countries of Thrace, Macedonia, and Greece, preserves the memory of their ancient state under the Roman empire. In the time of the Antonines the martial regions of Thrace, from the mountains of Hæmus and Rhodope to the Bosphorus and the Hellespont, had assumed the form of a province. Notwithstanding the change of masters and of religion, the new city of Rome, founded by Constantine on the banks of the Bosphorus, has ever since remained the capital of a great monarchy. The kingdom of Macedonia, which under the reign of Alexander gave laws to Asia, derived more solid advantages from the policy of the two Philips, and with its dependencies of Epirus and Thessaly extended from the Ægean to the Ionian Sea. When we reflect on the fame of Thebes and Argos, of Sparta and Athens, we can scarcely persuade ourselves that so many immortal republics of ancient Greece were lost in a single province of the Roman empire, which from the superior influence of the Achæan league was usually denominated the province of Achaia.

Such was the state of Europe under the Roman emperors. The provinces of Asia, without excepting the transient conquests of Trajan, are all comprehended within the limits of the Turkish power. But instead of following the arbitrary 19 divisions of despotism and ignorance, it will be safer for us, as well as more agreeable, to observe the indelible characters of nature. The name of Asia Minor is attributed with some propriety to the peninsula which, confined betwixt the Euxine and the Mediterranean, advances from the Euphrates towards Europe. The most extensive and flourishing district, westward of Mount Taurus and the river Halys, was dignified by the Romans with the exclusive title of Asia. The jurisdiction of that province extended over the ancient monarchies of Troy, Lydia, and Phrygia, the maritime countries of the Pamphylians, Lycians, and Carians, and the Grecian colonies of Ionia, which equalled in arts, though not in arms, the glory of their parent. The kingdoms of Bithynia and Pontus possessed the northern side of the peninsula from Constantinople to Trebizond. On the opposite side, the province of Cilicia was terminated by the mountains of Syria; the inland country, separated from the Roman Asia by the river Halys, and from Armenia by the Euphrates, had once formed the independent kingdom of Cappadocia. In this place we may observe that the northern shores of the Euxine, beyond Trebizond in Asia and beyond the Danube in Europe, acknowledged the sovereignty of the emperors and received at their hands either tributary princes or Roman garrisons. Budzak, Crim Tartary, Circassia and Mingrelia are the modern appellations of those savage countries.

Under the successors of Alexander, Syria was the seat of the Seleucidæ, who reigned over Upper Asia till the successful revolt of the Parthians confined their dominions between the Euphrates and the Mediterranean. When Syria became subject to the Romans it formed the eastern frontier of their empire; nor did that province, in its utmost latitude, know any other bounds than the mountains of Cappadocia to the north, and towards the south the confines of Eygpt and the Red Sea. Phœnicia and Palestine were sometimes annexed to, and sometimes separated from, the jurisdiction of Syria. The former of these was a narrow and rocky coast; the latter was a territory scarcely superior to Wales either in fertility or extent. Yet Phœnicia and Palestine will forever live in the memory of mankind, since America as well as Europe has received letters from the one and religion from the other. A sandy desert alike destitute of wood and water skirts along the doubtful confine of Syria from the Euphrates to the Red Sea. The wandering life of the Arabs was inseparably connected with their independence; and wherever, on some spots less barren than the rest, they ventured to form any settled habitation, they soon became subjects to the Roman empire.

The geographers of antiquity have frequently hesitated to what portion of the globe they should ascribe Egypt. By its situation that celebrated kingdom is included within the immense peninsula of Africa; but it is accessible only on the side of Asia, whose revolutions in almost every period of history Egypt has humbly obeyed. A Roman præfect was seated on the splendid throne of the Ptolemies, and the iron sceptre of the Mamalukes is now in the hands of a Turkish pasha. The Nile flows down the country, above five hundred miles from the Tropic of Cancer to the Mediterranean, and marks on either side the extent of fertility by the measure of its inundations. Cyrene, situate towards the west and along the seacoast, was first a Greek colony, afterwards a province of Egypt, and is now lost in the desert of Barca.

From Cyrene to the ocean the coast of Africa extends above fifteen hundred miles; yet so closely is it pressed between the Mediterranean and the Sahara, or sandy desert, that its breadth seldom exceeds fourscore or an hundred miles. The eastern division was considered by the Romans as the more peculiar and proper province of Africa. Till the arrival of the Phœnician colonies that fertile country was inhabited by the Libyans, the most savage of mankind. Under the immediate jurisdiction of Carthage it became the centre of commerce and empire; but the republic of Carthage is now degenerated into the feeble and disorderly states of Tripoli and Tunis. The military government of Algiers oppresses the wide extent of Numidia, as it was once united under Massinissa and Jugurtha; but in the time of Augustus the limits of Numidia were contracted, and at least two-thirds of the country acquiesced in the name of Mauritania, with the epithet of Cæsariensis. The genuine Mauritania, or country of the Moors, which from the ancient city of Tingi (or Tangier) was distinguished by the appellation of Tingitana, is represented by the modern kingdom of Fez. Sallè, on the ocean, long infamous for its piratical depredations, was noticed by the Romans as the extreme object of their power and almost of their geography. A city of their foundation may still be discovered near Mequinez, the residence of the barbarian whom we condescend to style the Emperor of Morocco; but it does not appear that his more southern dominions, Morocco itself, and Segelmessa, were ever comprehended within the Roman province. The western parts of Africa are intersected by the branches of Mount Atlas, a name so idly celebrated by the fancy of poets, but which is now diffused over the immense ocean that rolls between the ancient and the new continent.

Having now finished the circuit of the Roman empire, we may observe that Africa is divided from Spain by a narrow strait of about twelve miles, through which the Atlantic flows into the Mediterranean. The columns of Hercules, so famous among the ancients, were two mountains which seemed to have been torn asunder by some convulsion of the elements, and at the foot of the European mountain the fortress of Gibraltar is now seated. The whole extent of the Mediterranean Sea, its coasts, and its islands, were comprised within the Roman dominion. Of the larger islands the two Baleares, which derive their name of Majorca and Minorca from their respective size, are subject at present, the former to Spain, the latter to Great Britain. It is easier to deplore the fate than to describe the actual condition of Corsica. Two Italian sovereigns assume a regal title from Sardinia and Sicily. Crete, or Candia, with Cyprus, and most of the smaller islands of Greece and Asia, have been subdued by the Turkish arms; whilst the little rock of Malta defies their power and has emerged, under the government of its military Order, into fame and opulence.

This long enumeration of provinces, whose broken fragments have formed so many powerful kingdoms, might almost induce us to forgive the vanity or ignorance of the ancients. Dazzled with the extensive sway, the irresistible strength, and the real or affected moderation of the emperors, they permitted themselves to despise, and sometimes to forget, the outlying countries which had been left in the enjoyment of a barbarous independence; and they gradually usurped the license of confounding the Roman monarchy with the globe of the earth. But the temper as well as knowledge of a modern historian requires a more sober and accurate language. He may impress a juster image of the greatness of Rome by observing that the empire was above two thousand miles in breadth, from the wall of Antoninus and the northern limits of Dacia to Mount Atlas and the Tropic of Cancer; it extended in length more than three thousand miles from the Western Ocean to the Euphrates; it was situated in the finest part of the Temperate Zone, between the twenty-fourth and fifty-sixth degrees of northern latitude; and it was supposed to contain above sixteen hundred thousand square miles, for the most part of fertile and well-cultivated land.

II

Of the union and internal prosperity of the Roman empire in the age of the Antonines

It is not alone by the rapidity or extent of conquest that we should estimate the greatness of Rome. The sovereign of the Russian deserts commands a larger portion of the globe. In the seventh summer after his passage of the Hellespont, Alexander erected the Macedonian trophies on the banks of the Hyphasis. Within less than a century the irresistible Zingis and the Mogul princes of his race spread their cruel devastations and transient empire from the sea of China to the confines of Egypt and Germany. But the firm edifice of Roman power was raised and preserved by the wisdom of ages. The obedient provinces of Trajan and the Antonines were united by laws and adorned by arts. They might occasionally suffer from the partial abuse of delegated authority; but the general principle of government was wise, simple, and beneficent. They enjoyed the religion of their ancestors, whilst in civil honours and advantages they were exalted, by just degrees, to an equality with their conquerors.

The policy of the emperors and the senate, as far as it

concerned religion, was happily seconded by the reflections of the enlightened, and by the habits of the superstitious, part of their subjects. The various modes of worship which prevailed in the Roman world were all considered by the people as equally true, by the philosopher as equally false, and by the magistrate as equally useful. And thus toleration produced not only mutual indulgence but even religious concord.

The superstition of the people was not embittered by any mixture of theological rancour, nor was it confined by the chains of any speculative system. The devout polytheist, though fondly attached to his national rites, admitted with implicit faith the different religions of the earth. Fear, gratitude, and curiosity, a dream or an omen, a singular disorder or a distant journey, perpetually disposed him to multiply the articles of his belief and to enlarge the list of his protectors. The thin texture of the pagan mythology was interwoven with various but not discordant materials. As soon as it was allowed that sages and heroes who had lived or who had died for the benefit of their country were exalted to a state of power and immortality, it was universally confessed that they deserved, if not the adoration, at least the reverence, of all mankind. The deities of a thousand groves and a thousand streams possessed in peace their local and respective influence; nor could the Roman who deprecated the wrath of the Tiber deride the Egyptian who presented his offering to the beneficent genius of the Nile. The visible powers of Nature, the planets, and the elements were the same throughout the universe. The invisible governors of the moral world were inevitably cast in a similar mould of fiction and allegory. Every virtue, and even vice, acquired its divine representative, every art and profession its patron, whose attributes, in the most distant ages and countries, were uniformly derived from the character of their peculiar votaries. A republic of gods of such opposite tempers and interest required, in every system, the moderating hand of a supreme magistrate, who by the progress of knowledge and flattery was gradually invested with the sublime perfections of an Eternal Parent and an Omnipotent Monarch. Such was the mild spirit of antiquity that the nations were less attentive to the difference than to the resemblance of their religious worship. The Greek, the Roman, and the barbarian, as they met before their respective altars, easily persuaded themselves that under various names and with various ceremonies they adored the same deities. The elegant mythology of Homer gave a beautiful and almost a regular form to the polytheism of the ancient world.

The philosophers of Greece deduced their morals from the nature of man rather than from that of God. They meditated, however, on the Divine Nature as a very curious and important speculation; and in the profound inquiry they displayed the strength and weakness of the human understanding. Of the four most celebrated schools, the Stoics and the Platonists endeavoured to reconcile the jarring interests of reason and piety. They have left us the most sublime proofs of the existence and perfections of the first cause; but, as it was impossible for them to conceive the creation of matter, the workman in the Stoic philosophy was not sufficiently distinguished from the work; whilst, on the contrary, the spiritual God of Plato and his disciples resembled an idea rather than a substance. The opinions of the Academics and Epicureans were of a less religious cast; but whilst the modest science of the former induced them to doubt, the positive ignorance of the latter urged them to deny, the providence of a Supreme Ruler. The spirit of inquiry, prompted by emulation and supported by freedom, had divided the public teachers of philosophy into a variety of contending sects; but the ingenuous youth, who from every part resorted to Athens and the other seats of learning in the Roman empire, were alike instructed in every school to reject and to despise the religion of the multitude. How, indeed, was it possible that a philosopher should accept as divine truths the idle tales of the poets and the incoherent traditions of antiquity, or that he should adore as gods those imperfect beings whom he must have despised as men! Against such unworthy adversaries Cicero condescended to employ the arms of reason and eloquence, but the satire of Lucian was a much more adequate as well as more efficacious weapon. We may be well assured that a writer conversant with the world would never have ventured to expose the gods of his country to public ridicule had they not already been the objects of secret contempt among the polished and enlightened orders of society.

Notwithstanding the fashionable irreligion which prevailed in the age of the Antonines, both the interests of the priests and the credulity of the people were sufficiently respected. In their writings and conversation the philosophers of antiquity asserted the independent dignity of reason; but they resigned their actions to the commands of law and of custom. Viewing with a smile of pity and indulgence the various errors of the vulgar, they diligently practised the ceremonies of their fathers, devoutly frequented the temples of the gods; and sometimes condescending to act a part on the theatre of superstition, they concealed the sentiments of an atheist under the sacerdotal robes. Reasoners of such a temper were scarcely inclined to wrangle about their respective modes of faith or of worship. It was indifferent to them what shape the folly of the multitude might choose to assume; and they approached with the same inward contempt and the same external reverence the altars of the Libyan, the Olympian, or the Capitoline Jupiter.

It is not easy to conceive from what motives a spirit of persecution could introduce itself into the Roman councils. The magistrates could not be actuated by a blind though honest bigotry, since the magistrates were themselves philosophers; and the schools of Athens had given laws to the senate. They could not be impelled by ambition or avarice, as the temporal and ecclesiastical powers were united in the same hands. The pontiffs were chosen among the most illustrious of the senators, and the office of supreme pontiff was constantly exercised by the emperors themselves. They knew and valued the advantages of religion as it is connected with civil government. They encouraged the public festivals which humanize the manners of the people. They managed the arts of divination as a convenient instrument of policy; and they respected as the firmest bond of society the useful persuasion that, either in this or in a future life, the crime of perjury is most assuredly punished by the avenging gods. But whilst they acknowledged the general advantages of religion, they were convinced that the various modes of worship contributed alike to the same salutary purposes, and that in every country the form of superstition which had received the sanction of time and experience was the best adapted to the climate and to its inhabitants. Avarice and taste very frequently despoiled the vanquished nations of the elegant statues of their gods and the rich ornaments of their temples; but in the exercise of the religion which they derived from their ancestors they uniformly experienced the indulgence and even protection of the Roman conquerors. The province of Gaul seems, and indeed only seems, an exception to this universal toleration. Under the specious pretext of abolishing human sacrifices, the emperors Tiberius and Claudius suppressed the dangerous power of the Druids; but the priests themselves, their gods and their altars, subsisted in peaceful obscurity till the final destruction of paganism.

Rome, the capital of a great monarchy, was incessantly filled with subjects and strangers from every part of the world, who all introduced and enjoyed the favourite superstitions of their native country. Every city in the empire was justified in maintaining the purity of its ancient ceremonies; and the Roman senate, using the common privilege, sometimes interposed to check this inundation of foreign rites. The Egyptian superstition, of all the most contemptible and abject, was frequently prohibited, the temples of Serapis and Isis demolished, and their worshippers banished from Rome and Italy. But the zeal of fanaticism prevailed over the cold and feeble efforts of policy. The exiles returned, the proselytes multiplied, the temples were restored with increasing splendour, and Isis and Serapis at length assumed their place among the Roman deities. Nor was this indulgence a departure from the old maxims of government. In the purest ages of the commonwealth Cybele and Æsculapius had been invited by solemn embassies; and it was customary to tempt the protectors of besieged cities by the promise of more distinguished honours than they possessed in their native country. Rome gradually became the common temple of her subjects, and the freedom of the city was bestowed on all the gods of mankind.

The narrow policy of preserving, without any foreign mixture, the pure blood of the ancient citizens had checked the fortune and hastened the ruin of Athens and Sparta. The aspiring genius of Rome sacrificed vanity to ambition and deemed it more prudent as well as honourable to adopt virtue and merit for her own wheresoever they were found, among slaves or strangers, enemies or barbarians. During the most flourishing era of the Athenian commonwealth the number of citizens gradually decreased from about thirty to twenty-one thousand. If, on the contrary, we study the growth of the Roman republic, we may discover that, notwithstanding the incessant demands of war and colonies, the citizens who, in the first census of Servius Tullius, amounted to no more than eighty-three thousand were multiplied, before the commencement of the social war, to the number of four hundred and sixty-three thousand men able to bear arms in the service of their country. When the allies of Rome claimed an equal share of honours and privileges, the senate indeed preferred the chance of arms to an ignominious concession. The Samnites and the Lucanians paid the severe penalty of their rashness; but the rest of the Italian states, as they successively returned to their duty, were admitted into the bosom of the republic and soon contributed to the ruin of public freedom. Under a democratical government the citizens exercise the powers of sovereignty; and those powers will be first abused and afterwards lost if they are committed to an unwieldy multitude. But when the popular assemblies had been suppressed by the administration of the emperors, the conquerors were distinguished from the vanquished nations only as the first and most honourable order of subjects; and their increase, however rapid, was no longer exposed to the same dangers. Yet the wisest princes, who adopted the maxims of Augustus, guarded with the strictest care the dignity of the Roman name and diffused the freedom of the city with a prudent liberality.

Till the privileges of Romans had been progressively extended to all the inhabitants of the empire, an important distinction was preserved between Italy and the provinces. The former was esteemed the centre of public unity and the firm basis of the constitution. Italy claimed the birth, or at least the residence, of the emperors and the senate. The estates of the Italians were exempt from taxes, their persons from the arbitrary jurisdiction of governors. Their municipal corporations, formed after the perfect model of the capital, were entrusted, under the immediate eye of the supreme power, with the execution of the laws. From the foot of the Alps to the extremity of Calabria all the natives of Italy were born citizens of Rome. Their partial distinctions were obliterated, and they insensibly coalesced into one great nation, united by language, manners, and civil institutions, and equal to the weight of a powerful empire.

The provinces of the empire (as they have been described in the preceding chapter) were destitute of any public force or constitutional freedom. In Etruria, in Greece, and in Gaul, it was the first care of the senate to dissolve those dangerous confederacies which taught mankind that as the Roman arts prevailed by division they might be resisted by union. Those princes whom the ostentation of gratitude or generosity permitted for a while to hold a precarious sceptre were dismissed from their thrones as soon as they had performed their appointed task of fashioning to the yoke the vanquished nations. The free states and cities which had embraced the cause of Rome were rewarded with a nominal alliance and insensibly sunk into real servitude. The public authority was everywhere exercised by the ministers of the senate and of the emperors, and that authority was absolute and without control. But the same salutary maxims of government which had secured the peace and obedience of Italy were extended to the most distant conquests. A nation of Romans was gradually formed in the provinces by the double expedient of introducing colonies and of admitting the most faithful and deserving of the provincials to the freedom of Rome.

'Wheresoever the Roman conquers, he inhabits,' is a very just observation of Seneca, confirmed by history and experience. The natives of Italy, allured by pleasure or by interest, hastened to enjoy the advantages of victory; and we may remark that about forty years after the reduction of Asia eighty thousand Romans were massacred in one day by the cruel orders of Mithridates. These voluntary exiles were engaged for the most part in the occupations of commerce, agriculture, and the farm of the revenue. But after the legions were rendered permanent by the emperors, the provinces were peopled by a race of soldiers; and the veterans, whether they received the reward of their service in land or in money, usually settled with their families in the country where they had honourably spent their youth. Throughout the empire, but more particularly in the western parts, the most fertile districts and the most convenient situations were reserved for the establishment of colonies, some of which were of a civil and others of a military nature.

So sensible were the Romans of the influence of language over national manners that it was their most serious care to extend, with the progress of their arms, the use of the Latin tongue. The ancient dialects of Italy, the Sabine, the Etruscan, and the Venetian, sunk into oblivion; but in the provinces the east was less docile than the west to the voice of its victorious preceptors. This obvious difference marked the two portions of the empire with a distinction of colours which, though it was in some degree concealed during the meridian splendour of prosperity, became gradually more visible as the shades of night descended upon the Roman world. The western countries were civilized by the same hands which subdued them. As soon as the barbarians were reconciled to obedience, their minds were opened to any new impressions of knowledge and politeness. The language of Virgil and Cicero, though with some inevitable mixture of corruption, was so universally adopted in Africa, Spain, Gaul, Britain, and Pannonia that the faint traces of the Punic or Celtic idioms were preserved only in the mountains or among the peasants. Education and study insensibly inspired the natives of those countries with the sentiments of Romans; and Italy gave fashions as well as laws to her Latin provincials. They solicited with more ardour, and obtained with more facility, the freedom and honours of the state, supported the national dignity in letters and in arms, and at length, in the person of Trajan, produced an emperor whom the Scipios would not have disowned for their countryman.

The situation of the Greeks was very different from that of the barbarians. The former had been long since civilized and corrupted. They had too much taste to relinquish their language, and too much vanity to adopt any foreign institutions. Still preserving the prejudices after they had lost the virtues of their ancestors, they affected to despise the unpolished manners of the Roman conquerors whilst they were compelled to respect their superior wisdom and power. Nor was the influence of the Grecian language and sentiments confined to the narrow limits of that once celebrated country. Their empire, by the progress of colonies and conquest, had been diffused from the Hadriatic to the Euphrates and the Nile. Asia was covered with Greek cities, and the long reign of the Macedonian kings had introduced a silent revolution into Syria and Egypt. In their pompous courts those princes united the elegance of Athens with the luxury of the East; and the example of the court was imitated at an humble distance by the higher ranks of their subjects. Such was the general division of the Roman empire into the Latin and Greek languages. To these we may add a third distinction for the body of the natives in Syria and especially in Egypt. The use of their ancient dialects, by secluding them from the commerce of mankind, checked the improvements of those barbarians. The slothful effeminacy of the former exposed them to the contempt, the sullen ferociousness of the latter excited the aversion, of the conquerors. Those nations had submitted to the Roman power, but they seldom desired or deserved the freedom of the city; and it was remarked that more than two hundred and thirty years elapsed after the ruin of the Ptolemies before an Egyptian was admitted into the senate of Rome.

It is a just though trite observation that victorious Rome was herself subdued by the arts of Greece. Those immortal writers who still command the admiration of modern Europe soon became the favourite object of study and imitation in Italy and the western provinces. But the elegant amusements of the Romans were not suffered to interfere with their sound maxims of policy. Whilst they acknowledged the charms of the Greek, they asserted the dignity of the Latin tongue, and the exclusive use of the latter was inflexibly maintained in the administration of civil as well as military government. The two languages exercised at the same time their separate jurisdiction throughout the empire, the former as the natural idiom of science, the latter as the legal dialect of public transactions. Those who united letters with business were equally conversant with both; and it was almost impossible in any province to find a Roman subject of a liberal education who was at once a stranger to the Greek and to the Latin language.

It was by such institutions that the nations of the empire insensibly melted away into the Roman name and people. But there still remained, in the centre of every province and of every family, an unhappy condition of men who endured the weight, without sharing the benefits, of society. In the free states of antiquity the domestic slaves were exposed to the wanton rigour of despotism. The perfect settlement of the Roman empire was preceded by ages of violence and rapine. The slaves consisted for the most part of barbarian captives, taken in thousands by the chance of war, purchased at a vile price, accustomed to a life of independence, and impatient to break and to revenge their fetters. Against such internal enemies, whose desperate insurrections had more than once reduced the republic to the brink of destruction, the most severe regulations and the most cruel treatment seemed almost justified by the great law of self-preservation. But when the principal nations of Europe, Asia, and Africa were united under the laws of one sovereign, the source of foreign supplies flowed with much less abundance, and the Romans were reduced to the milder but more tedious method of propagation. In their numerous families, and particularly in their country estates, they encouraged the marriage of their slaves. The sentiments of nature, the habits of education, and the possession of a dependent species of property contributed to alleviate the hardships of servitude. The existence of a slave became an object of greater value, and though his happiness still depended on the temper and circumstances of the master, the humanity of the latter, instead of being restrained by fear, was encouraged by the sense of his own interest. The

progress of manners was accelerated by the virtue or policy

of the emperors; and by the edicts of Hadrian and the Antonines the protection of the laws was extended to the most abject part of mankind. The jurisdiction of life and death over the slaves, a power long exercised and often abused, was taken out of private hands and reserved to the magistrates alone. The subterraneous prisons were abolished, and, upon a just complaint of intolerable treatment, the injured slave obtained either his deliverance or a less cruel master.

Hope, the best comfort of our imperfect condition, was not denied to the Roman slave; and if he had any opportunity of rendering himself either useful or agreeable, he might very naturally expect that the diligence and fidelity of a few years would be rewarded with the inestimable gift of freedom. The benevolence of the master was so frequently prompted by the meaner suggestions of vanity and avarice that the laws found it more necessary to restrain than to encourage a profuse and undistinguishing liberality, which might degenerate into a very dangerous abuse. It was a maxim of ancient jurisprudence that, [as] a slave had not any country of his own, he acquired with his liberty an admission into the political society of which his patron was a member. The consequences of this maxim would have prostituted the privileges of the Roman city to a mean and promiscuous multitude. Some seasonable exceptions were therefore provided; and the honourable distinction was confined to such slaves only as for just causes, and with the approbation of the magistrate, should receive a solemn and legal manumission. Even these chosen freedmen obtained no more than the private rights of citizens, and were rigorously excluded from civil or military honours. Whatever might be the merit or fortune of their sons, *they* likewise were esteemed unworthy of a seat in the senate; nor were the traces of a servile origin allowed to be completely obliterated till the third of fourth generation. Without destroying the distinction of ranks, the distant prospect of freedom and honours was presented even to those whom pride and prejudice almost disdained to number among the human species.

It was once proposed to discriminate the slaves by a peculiar habit; but it was just apprehended that there might be some danger in acquainting them with their own numbers. Without interpreting in their utmost strictness the liberal appellations of legions and myriads, we may venture to pronounce that the proportion of slaves, who were valued as property, was more considerable than that of servants, who can be computed only as an expense. The youths of a promising genius were instructed in the arts and sciences, and their price was ascertained by the dgree of their skill and talents. Almost every profession, either liberal or mechanical, might be found in the household of an opulent senator. The ministers of pomp and sensuality were multiplied beyond the conception of modern luxury. It was more for the interest of the merchant or manufacturer to purchase than to hire his workmen; and in the country slaves were employed as the cheapest and most laborious instruments of agriculture. To confirm the general observation and to display the multitude of slaves, we might allege a variety of particular instances. It was discovered, on a very melancholy occasion, that four hundred slaves were maintained in a single palace of Rome. The same number of four hundred belonged to an estate which an African widow, of a very private condition, resigned to her son, whilst she reserved for herself a much larger share of her property. A freedman under the reign of Augustus, though his fortune had suffered great losses in the civil wars, left behind him three thousand six hundred yoke of oxen, two hundred and fifty thousand head of smaller cattle, and, what was almost included in the description of cattle, four thousand one hundred and sixteen slaves.

The number of subjects who acknowledged the laws of Rome, of citizens, of provincials, and of slaves, cannot now be fixed with such a degree of accuracy as the importance of the object would deserve. We are informed that when the emperor Claudius exercised the office of censor, he took an account of six million nine hundred and forty-five thousand Roman citizens, who, with the proportion of women and children, must have amounted to about twenty millions of souls. The multitude of subjects of an inferior rank was uncertain and fluctuating. But after weighing with attention every circumstance which could influence the balance, it seems probable that there existed in the time of Claudius about twice as many provincials as there were citizens, of either sex and of every age, and that the slaves were at least equal in number to the free inhabitants of the Roman world. The total amount of this imperfect calculation would rise to about one hundred and twenty millions of persons, a degree of population which possibly exceeds that of modern Europe and forms the most numerous society that has ever been united under the same system of government.

Domestic peace and union were the natural consequences of the moderate and comprehensive policy embraced by the Romans. If we turn our eyes towards the monarchies of Asia, we shall behold despotism in the centre and weakness in the extremities, the collection of the revenue or the administration of justice enforced by the presence of an army, hostile barbarians established in the heart of the country, hereditary satraps usurping the dominion of the provinces, and subjects inclined to rebellion though incapable of freedom. But the obedience of the Roman world was uniform, voluntary, and permanent. The vanquished nations, blended into one great people, resigned the hope, nay even the wish, of resuming their independence, and scarcely considered their own existence as distinct from the existence of Rome. The established authority of the emperors pervaded without an effort the wide extent of their dominions and was exercised with the same facility on the banks of the Thames or of the Nile as on those of the Tiber. The legions were destined to serve against the public enemy, and the civil magistrate seldom required the aid of a military force. In this state of general security the leisure as well as opulence both of the prince and people were devoted to improve and to adorn the Roman empire.

Among the innumerable monuments of architecture constructed by the Romans, how many have escaped the notice of history, how few have resisted the ravages of time and barbarism! And yet even the majestic ruins that are still scattered over Italy and the provinces would be sufficient to prove that those countries were once the seat of a polite and powerful empire. Their greatness alone, or their beauty, might deserve our attention; but they are rendered more interesting by two important circumstances, which connect the agreeable history of the arts with the more useful history of human manners. Many of those works were erected at private expense, and almost all were intended for public benefit.

It is natural to suppose that the greatest number, as well as the most considerable, of the Roman edifices were raised by the emperors, who possessed so unbounded a command both of men and money. Augustus was accustomed to boast that he had found his capital of brick and that he had left it of marble. The strict economy of Vespasian was the source of his magnificence. The works of Trajan bear the stamp of his genius. The public monuments with which Hadrian adorned every province of the empire were executed not only by his orders, but under his immediate inspection. He was himself an artist; and he loved the arts, as they conduced to the glory of the monarch. They were encouraged by the Antonines, as they contributed to the happiness of the people. But if the emperors were the first, they were not the only architects of their dominions. Their example was universally imitated by their principal subjects, who were not afraid of declaring to the world that they had spirit to conceive and wealth to accomplish the noblest undertakings. Scarcely had the proud structure of the Coliseum been dedicated at Rome before the edifices of a smaller scale, indeed, but of the same design and materials, were erected for the use and at the expense of the cities of Capua and Verona. The inscription of the stupendous bridge of Alcantara attests that it was thrown over the Tagus by the contribution of a few Lusitanian communities. When Pliny was entrusted with the government of Bithynia and Pontus, provinces by no means the richest or most considerable of the empire, he found the cities within his jurisdiction striving with each other in every useful and ornamental work that might deserve the curiosity of strangers or the gratitude of their citizens. It was the duty of the proconsul to supply their deficiencies, to direct their taste, and sometimes to moderate their emulation. The opulent senators of Rome and the provinces esteemed it an honour, and almost an obligation, to adorn the splendour of their age and country; and the influence of fashion very frequently supplied the want of taste or generosity. Among a crowd of these private benefactors we may select Herodes Atticus, an Athenian citizen who lived in the age of the Antonines. Whatever might be the motive of his conduct, his magnificence would have been worthy of the greatest kings.

The family of Herod, at least after it had been favoured by fortune, was lineally descended from Cimon and Miltiades, Theseus and Cecrops, Æacus and Jupiter. But the posterity of so many gods and heroes was fallen into the most abject state. His grandfather had suffered by the hands of justice; and Julius Atticus, his father, must have ended his life in poverty and contempt had he not discovered an immense treasure buried under an old house, the last remains of his patrimony. According to the rigour of law, the emperor might have asserted his claim, and the prudent Atticus prevented, by a frank confession, the officiousness of informers. But the equitable Nerva, who then filled the throne, refused to accept any part of it and commanded him to use without scruple the present of fortune. The cautious Athenian still insisted that the treasure was too considerable for a subject and that he knew not how to *use it*. *Abuse it, then*, replied the monarch with a good-natured peevishness, *for it is your own*. Many will be of opinion that Atticus literally obeyed the emperor's last instructions, since he expended the greatest part of his fortune, which was much increased by an advantageous marriage, in the service of the public. He had obtained for his son Herod the præfecture of the free cities of Asia; and the young magistrate, observing that the town of Troas was indifferently supplied with water, obtained from the munificence of Hadrian three hundred myriads of drachms (about a hundred thousand pounds) for the construction of a new aqueduct. But in the execution of the work the charge amounted to more than double the estimate, and the officers of the revenue began to murmur, till the generous Atticus silenced their complaints by requesting that he might be permitted to take upon himself the whole additional expense.

The ablest preceptors of Greece and Asia had been invited by liberal rewards to direct the education of young Herod. Their pupil soon became a celebrated orator according to the useless rhetoric of that age, which, confining itself to the schools, disdained to visit either the Forum or the senate. He was honoured with the consulship at Rome; but the greatest part of his life was spent in a philosophic retirement at Athens and his adjacent villas, perpetually surrounded by sophists, who acknowledged without reluctance the superiority of a rich and generous rival. The monuments of his genius have perished; [but] some considerable ruins still preserve the fame of his taste and munificence, [and] modern travellers have measured the remains of the stadium which he constructed at Athens. It was six hundred feet in length, built entirely of white marble, capable of admitting the whole body of the people, and finished in four years whilst Herod was president of the Athenian games. To the memory of his wife Regilla he dedicated a theatre scarcely to be paralleled in the empire; no wood except cedar, very curiously carved, was employed in any part of the building. The Odeum, designed by Pericles for musical performances and the rehearsal of new tragedies, had been a trophy of the victory of the arts over barbaric greatness, as the timbers employed in the construction consisted chiefly of the masts of the Persian vessels. Notwithstanding the repairs bestowed on that ancient edifice by a king of Cappadocia, it was again fallen to decay. Herod restored its ancient beauty and magnificence. Nor was the liberality of that illustrious citizen confined to the walls of Athens. The most splendid ornaments bestowed on the temple of Neptune in the Isthmus, a theatre at Corinth, a stadium at Delphi, a bath at Thermopylæ, and an aqueduct at Canusium in Italy were insufficient to exhaust his treasures. The people of Epirus, Thessaly, Eubœa, Bœotia, and Peloponnesus experienced his favours, and many inscriptions of the cities of Greece and Asia gratefully style Herodes Atticus their patron and benefactor.

In the commonwealths of Athens and Rome the modest simplicity of private houses announced the equal condition of freedom, whilst the sovereignty of the people was represented in the majestic edifices destined to the public use; nor was this republican spirit totally extinguished by the introduction of wealth and monarchy. It was in works of national honour and benefit that the most virtuous of the emperors affected to display their magnificence. The golden palace of Nero excited a just indignation, but the vast extent of ground which had been usurped by his selfish luxury was more nobly filled under the succeeding reigns by the

Coliseum, the baths of Titus, the Claudian portico, and the temples dedicated to the goddess of Peace and to the genius of Rome. These monuments of architecture, the property of the Roman people, were adorned with the most beautiful productions of Grecian painting and sculpture; and in the temple of Peace a very curious library was open to the curiosity of the learned. At a small distance from thence was situated the Forum of Trajan. It was surrounded with a lofty portico, in the form of a quadrangle, into which four triumphal arches opened a noble and spacious entrance; in the centre arose a column of marble, whose height of one hundred and ten feet denoted the elevation of the hill that had been cut away. This column, which still subsists in its ancient beauty, exhibited an exact representation of the Dacian victories of its founder. The veteran soldier contemplated the story of his own campaigns, and by an easy illusion of national vanity, the peaceful citizen associated himself to the honours of the triumph.

All the other quarters of the capital and all the provinces of the empire were embellished by the same liberal spirit of public magnificence, and were filled with amphitheatres, theatres, temples, porticos, triumphal arches, baths, and aqueducts, all variously conducive to the health, the devotion, and the pleasures of the meanest citizen. The last mentioned of those edifices deserve our peculiar attention. The boldness of the enterprise, the solidity of the execution, and the uses to which they were subservient rank the aqueducts among the noblest monuments of Roman genius and power. The aqueducts of the capital claim a just pre-eminence; but the curious traveller who, without the light of history, should examine those of Spoleto, of Metz, or of Segovia would very naturally conclude that those provincial towns had formerly been the residence of some potent monarch. The solitudes of Asia and Africa were once covered with flourishing cities, whose populousness and even whose existence was derived from such artificial supplies of a perennial stream of fresh water.

We have computed the inhabitants and contemplated the public works of the Roman empire. The observation of the number and greatness of its cities will serve to confirm the former and to multiply the latter. It may not be unpleasing to collect a few scattered instances relative to that subject, without forgetting, however, that from the vanity of nations and the poverty of language the vague appellation of city has been indifferently bestowed on Rome and upon Laurentum. *Ancient* Italy is said to have contained eleven hundred and ninety-seven cities; and for whatsoever era of antiquity the expression might be intended, there is not any reason to believe that country less populous in the age of the Antonines than in that of Romulus. The petty states of Latium were contained within the metropolis of the empire, by whose superior influence they had been attracted. Those parts of Italy which have so long languished under the lazy tyranny of priests and viceroys had been afflicted only by the more tolerable calamities of war; and the first symptoms of decay which *they* experienced were amply compensated by the rapid improvements of the Cisalpine Gaul. The splendour of Verona may be traced in its remains; yet Verona was less celebrated than Aquileia or Padua, Milan or Ravenna.

The spirit of improvement had passed the Alps and been felt even in the woods of Britain, which were gradually cleared away to open a free space for convenient and elegant habitations. York was the seat of government; London was already enriched by commerce; and Bath was celebrated for the salutary effects of its medicinal waters. Gaul could boast of her twelve hundred cities; and though in the northern parts many of them, without excepting Paris itself, were little more than the rude and imperfect townships of a rising people, the southern provinces imitated the wealth and elegance of Italy. Many were the cities of Gaul – Marseilles, Arles, Nîmes, Narbonne, Toulouse, Bordeaux, Autun, Vienna, Lyons, Langres and Treves – whose ancient condition might sustain an equal and perhaps advantageous comparison with their present state. With regard to Spain, that country flourished as a province and has declined as a kingdom. Exhausted by the abuse of her strength, by America, and by superstition, her pride might possibly be confounded if we required such a list of three hundred and sixty cities as Pliny has exhibited under the reign of Vespasian.

Three hundred African cities had once acknowledged the authority of Carthage, nor is it likely that their numbers diminished under the administration of the emperors.

Carthage itself rose with new splendour from its ashes; and that capital, as well as Capua and Corinth, soon recovered all the advantages which can be separated from independent sovereignty. The provinces of the East present the contrast of Roman magnificence with Turkish barbarism. The ruins of antiquity scattered over uncultivated fields, and ascribed by ignorance to the power of magic, scarcely afford a shelter to the oppressed peasant or wandering Arab. Under the reign of the Cæsars the proper Asia alone contained five hundred populous cities, enriched with all the gifts of Nature and adorned with all the refinements of art. Eleven cities of Asia had once disputed the honour of dedicating a temple to Tiberius, and their respective merits were examined by the senate. Four of them were immediately rejected as unequal to the burden; and among these was Laodicea, whose splendour is still displayed in its ruins. Laodicea collected a very considerable revenue from its flocks of sheep, celebrated for the fineness of their wool, and had received, a little before the contest, a legacy of above four hundred thousand pounds by the testament of a generous citizen. If such was the poverty of Laodicea, what must have been the wealth of those cities whose claim appeared preferable, and particularly of Pergamus, of Smyrna, and of Ephesus, who so long disputed with each other over the titular primacy of Asia. The capitals of Syria and Egypt held a still superior rank in the empire: Antioch and Alexandria looked down with disdain on a crowd of dependent cities, and yielded with reluctance to the majesty 51 of Rome itself.

All these cities were connected with each other and with the capital by the public highways which, issuing from the Forum of Rome, traversed Italy, pervaded the provinces, and were terminated only by the frontiers of the empire. If we carefully trace the distance from the wall of Antoninus to Rome, and from thence to Jerusalem, it will be found that the great chain of communication from the northwest to the southeast point of the empire was drawn out to the length of four thousand and eighty Roman miles. The public roads were accurately divided by milestones and ran in a direct line from one city to another with very little respect for the obstacles either of nature or private property. Mountains were perforated, and bold arches thrown over the broadest and most rapid streams. The middle part of the road was raised into a terrace which commanded the adjacent country, consisted of several strata of sand, gravel, and cement, and was paved with large stones or, in some places near the capital, with granite.

Such was the solid construction of the Roman highways, whose firmness has not entirely yielded to the effort of fifteen centuries. They united the subjects of the most distant provinces by an easy and familiar intercourse, but their primary object had been to facilitate the marches of the legions; nor was any country considered as completely subdued till it had been rendered, in all its parts, pervious to the arms and authority of the conqueror. The advantage of receiving the earliest intelligence, and of conveying their orders with celerity, induced the emperors to establish throughout their extensive dominions the regular institution of posts. Houses were everywhere erected at the distance only of five or six miles; each of them was constantly provided with forty houses; and by the help of these relays it was easy to travel an hundred miles in a day along the Roman roads. The use of the posts was allowed to those who claimed it by an Imperial mandate; but though originally intended for the public service, it was sometimes indulged to the business or conveniency of private citizens. Nor was the communication of the Roman empire less free and open by sea than it was by land. The provinces surrounded and enclosed the Mediterranean; and Italy, in the shape of an immense promontory, advanced into the midst of that great lake. The coasts of Italy are in general destitute of safe harbours, but human industry had corrected the deficiencies of nature; and the artificial port of Ostia in particular, situate at the mouth of the Tiber and formed by the emperor Claudius, was a useful monument of Roman greatness. From this port, which was only sixteen miles from the capital, a favourable breeze frequently carried vessels in seven days to the columns of Hercules, and in nine or ten to Alexandria in Egypt.

Whatever evils either reason or declamation has imputed to extensive empire, the power of Rome was attended with some beneficial consequences to mankind; and the same freedom of intercourse which extended the vices diffused likewise the improvements of social life. In the more remote ages of antiquity the world was unequally divided. The East was in the immemorial possession of arts and luxury, whilst the West was inhabited by rude and warlike barbarians who either disdained agriculture or to whom it was totally unknown. Under the protection of an established government the productions of happier climates and the industry of more civilized nations were gradually introduced into the western countries of Europe; and the natives were encouraged, by an open and profitable commerce, to multiply the former as well as to improve the latter. It would be almost impossible to enumerate all the articles, either of the animal or the vegetable reign, which were successively imported into Europe from Asia and Egypt; but it will not be unworthy of the dignity, and much less of the utility, of a historical work slightly to touch on a few of the principal heads.

1. Almost all the flowers, the herbs, and the fruits that grow in our European gardens are of foreign extraction, which in many cases is betrayed even by their names. The apple was a native of Italy, and when the Romans had tasted the richer flavour of the apricot, the peach, the pomegranate, the citron, and the orange, they contented themselves with applying to all these new fruits the common denomination of apple, discriminating them from each other by the additional epithet of their country.

2. In the time of Homer the vine grew wild in the island of Sicily and most probably in the adjacent continent; but it was not improved by the skill, nor did it afford a liquor

grateful to the taste, of the savage inhabitants. A thousand years afterwards Italy could boast that of the fourscore most generous and celebrated wines, more than two-thirds were produced from her soil. The blessing was soon communicated to the Narbonnese province of Gaul; but so intense was the cold to the north of the Cevennes that, in the time of Strabo, it was thought impossible to ripen the grapes in those parts of Gaul. This difficulty, however, was gradually vanquished; and there is some reason to believe that the vineyards of Burgundy are as old as the age of the Antonines. The olive in the western world followed the progress of peace, of which it was considered as the symbol. Two centuries after the foundation of Rome both Italy and Africa were strangers to that useful plant; it was naturalized in those countries, and at length carried into the heart of Spain and Gaul. The timid errors of the ancients, that it required a certain degree of heat and could only flourish in the neighbourhood of the sea, were insensibly exploded by industry and experience. The cultivation of flax was transported from Egypt to Gaul and enriched the whole country, however it might impoverish the particular lands on which it was sown.

3. The use of artificial grasses became familiar to the farmers both of Italy and the provinces, particularly the Lucerne, which derived its name and origin from Media. The assured supply of wholesome and plentiful food for the cattle during winter multiplied the number of the flocks and herds, which in their turn contributed to the fertility of the

soil. To all these improvements may be added an assiduous attention to mines and fisheries, which, by employing a multitude of laborious hands, serve to increase the pleasures of the rich and the subsistence of the poor. The elegant treatise of Columella describes the advanced state of the Spanish husbandry under the reign of Tiberius; and it may be observed that those famines which so frequently afflicted the infant republic were seldom or never experienced by the extensive empire of Rome. The accidental scarcity in any single province was immediately relieved by the plenty of its more fortunate neighbours.

Agriculture is the foundation of manufactures, since the productions of nature are the materials of art. Under the Roman empire the labour of an industrious and ingenious people was variously but incessantly employed in the service of the rich. In their dress, their table, their houses, and their furniture, the favourites of fortune united every refinement of conveniency, of elegance, and of splendour, whatever could soothe their pride or gratify their sensuality. Such refinements, under the odious name of luxury, have been severely arraigned by the moralists of every age; and it might perhaps be more conducive to the virtue as well as happiness of mankind if all possessed the necessities, and none the superfluities, of life. But in the present imperfect condition of society, luxury, though it may proceed from vice or folly, seems to be the only means that can correct the unequal distribution of property. The diligent mechanic and the skilful artist, who have obtained no share in the division of the earth, receive a voluntary tax from the possessors of land; and the latter are prompted, by a sense of interest, to improve those estates with whose produce they may purchase additional pleasures. This operation, the particular effects of which are felt in every society, acted with much more diffusive energy in the Roman world. The provinces would soon have been exhausted of their wealth if the manufactures and commerce of luxury had not insensibly restored to the industrious subjects the sums which were exacted from them by the arms and authority of Rome. As long as the circulation was confined within the bounds of the empire it impressed the political machine with a new degree of activity, and its consequences, sometimes beneficial, could never become pernicious.

But it is no easy task to confine luxury within the limits of an empire. The most remote countries of the ancient world were ransacked to supply the pomp and delicacy of Rome. The forests of Scythia afforded some valuable furs. Amber was brought overland from the shores of the Baltic to the Danube, and the barbarians were astonished at the price which they received in exchange for so useless a commodity. There was a considerable demand for Babylonian carpets and other manufactures of the East; but the most important and unpopular branch of foreign trade was carried on with Arabia and India. Every year, about the time of the summer solstice, a fleet of a hundred and twenty vessels sailed from Myos-hormos, a port of Egypt on the Red Sea. By the periodical assistance of the monsoons they traversed the ocean in about forty days. The coast of Malabar or the island of Ceylon was the usual term of their navigation, and it was in those markets that the merchants from the more remote countries of Asia expected their arrival. The return of the fleet of Egypt was fixed to the months of December or January; and as soon as their rich cargo had been transported on the backs of camels from the Red Sea to the Nile, and had descended that river as far as Alexandria, it was poured without delay into the capital of the empire.

The objects of oriental traffic were splendid and trifling: silk, a pound of which was esteemed not inferior in value to a pound of gold; precious stones, among which the pearl claimed the first rank after the diamond; and a variety of aromatics that were consumed in religious worship and the pomp of funerals. The labour and risk of the voyage were rewarded with almost incredible profit; but the profit was made upon Roman subjects, and a few individuals were enriched at the expense of the public. As the natives of Arabia and India were contented with the productions and manufactures of their own country, silver, on the side of the Romans, was the principal if not the only instrument of commerce. It was a complaint worthy of the gravity of the senate that in the purchase of female ornaments the wealth of the state was irrevocably given away to foreign and hostile nations. The annual loss is computed, by a writer [Pliny] of an inquisitive but censorious temper, at upwards of eight hundred thousand pounds sterling. Such was the style of discontent, brooding over the dark prospect of approaching poverty. And yet, if we compare the proportion between gold and silver as it stood in the time of Pliny and as it was fixed in the reign of Constantine, we shall discover within that period a very considerable increase. There is not the least reason to suppose that gold was become more scarce: it is therefore evident that silver was grown more common; that whatever might be the amount of the Indian and Arabian exports, they were far from exhausting the wealth of the Roman world; and that the produce of the mines abundantly supplied the demands of commerce.

Notwithstanding the propensity of mankind to exalt the past and to depreciate the present, the tranquil and prosperous state of the empire was warmly felt and honestly confessed by the provincials as well as Romans. 'They acknowledged that the true principles of social life, laws, agriculture, and science, which had been first invented by the wisdom of Athens, were now firmly established by the power of Rome, under whose auspicious influence the fiercest barbarians were united by an equal government and common language. They affirm that with the improvement of arts, the human species was visibly multiplied. They celebrate the increasing splendour of the cities, the beautiful face of the country, cultivated and adorned like an immense garden; and the long festival of peace, which was enjoyed by so many nations, forgetful of their ancient animosities, and delivered from the apprehension of future danger.' Whatever suspicions may be suggested by the air of rhetoric and declamation which seems to prevail in these passages, the substance of them is perfectly agreeable to historic truth.

It was scarcely possible that the eyes of contemporaries should discover in the public felicity the latent causes of decay and corruption. This long peace, and the uniform government of the Romans, introduced a slow and secret poison into the vitals of the empire. The minds of men were gradually reduced to the same level, the fire of genius was extinguished, and even the military spirit evaporated. The natives of Europe were brave and robust; Spain, Gaul, Britain, and Illyricum supplied the legions with excellent soldiers and constituted the real strength of the monarchy. Their personal valour remained, but they no longer possessed that public courage which is nourished by the love of independence, the sense of national honour, the presence of danger, and the habit of command. They received laws and governors from the will of their sovereign and trusted for their defence to a mercenary army. The posterity of their boldest leaders was contented with the rank of citizens and subjects. The most aspiring spirits resorted to the court or standard of the emperors; and the deserted provinces, deprived of political strength or union, insensibly sank into the languid indifference of private life.

The love of letters, almost inseparable from peace and refinement, was fashionable among the subjects of Hadrian and the Antonines, who were themselves men of learning and curiosity. It was diffused over the whole extent of their empire; the most northern tribes of Britons had acquired a taste for rhetoric; Homer as well as Virgil were transcribed and studied on the banks of the Rhine and Danube; and the most liberal rewards sought out the faintest glimmerings of literary merit. The sciences of physic and astronomy were successfully cultivated by the Greeks; the observations of Ptolemy and the writings of Galen are studied by those who have improved their discoveries and corrected their errors; but if we except the inimitable Lucian, this age of indolence passed away without having produced a single writer of original genius or who excelled in the arts of elegant composition. The authority of Plato and Aristotle, of Zeno and Epicurus, still reigned in the schools; and their systems, transmitted with blind deference from one generation of disciples to another, precluded every generous attempt to exercise the powers or enlarge the limits of the human mind. The beauties of the poets and orators, instead of kindling a fire like their own, inspired only cold and servile imitations; or if any ventured to deviate from those models, they deviated at the same time from good sense and propriety. On the revival of letters, the youthful vigour of the imagination after a long repose, national emulation, a new religion, new languages, and a new world, called forth the genius of Europe. But the provincials of Rome, trained by a uniform artificial foreign education, were engaged in a very unequal competition with those bold ancients who, by expressing their genuine feelings in their native tongue, had already occupied every place of honour. The name of Poet was almost forgotten, that of Orator was usurped by the sophists. A cloud of critics, of compilers, of commentators, darkened the face of learning, and the decline of genius was soon followed by the corruption of taste.

The sublime Longinus, who in somewhat a later period and in the court of a Syrian queen preserved the spirit of ancient Athens, observes and laments this degeneracy of his contemporaries, which debased their sentiments, enervated their courage, and depressed their talents. 'In the same manner,' says he, 'as some children always remain pygmies, whose infant limbs have been too closely confined; thus our tender minds, fettered by the prejudices and habits of a just servitude, are unable to expand themselves, or to attain that well-proportioned greatness which we admire in the ancients who, living under a popular government, wrote with the same freedom as they acted.' This diminutive stature of mankind, if we pursue the metaphor, was daily sinking below the old standard; and the Roman world was indeed peopled by a race of pygmies when the fierce giants of the north broke in and mended the puny breed. They restored a manly spirit of freedom; and after the revolution of ten centuries, freedom became the happy parent of taste and science.